Anne Savarino is an aspiring, established author with Austin Macauley Publishers. Anne's versatility in writing both fiction and non-fiction romance, and health and well-being novel allows her to inspire and encourage people to reach their highest potential toward attaining their goals and especially finding true love and happiness in life.

I dedicate this book to my loving, wonderful husband, Vince. My true soul mate who has made my life complete and full of true love and happiness.

Anne Savarino

FOREVER TRUE LOVE

AUSTIN MACAULEY PUBLISHERS™

LONDON • CAMBRIDGE • NEW YORK • SHARJAH

Ordering Information
Quantity sales: Special discounts are available on quantity purchases by corporations, associations, and others. For details, contact the publisher at the address below.

Publisher's Cataloging-in-Publication data
Savarino, Anne
Forever True Love

ISBN 9798889109259 (Paperback)
ISBN 9798889109266 (Hardback)
ISBN 9798889109273 (ePub e-book)

Library of Congress Control Number: 2023918106

www.austinmacauley.com/us

First Published 2024
Austin Macauley Publishers LLC
40 Wall Street, 33rd Floor, Suite 3302
New York, NY 10005
USA

mail-usa@austinmacauley.com
+1 (646) 5125767

I would like to thank Austin Macauley Publishers and their wonderful staff in publishing my book *Forever True Love*. The exceptional work ethics Austin Macauley provides their clients with are of the highest form of excellence in professional standards. I am very happy to be working and collaborating with them on publishing my book and on any future endeavors.

Upbringings

I was born in 1951, where family value, love, and respect for each other was the most important aspect in our family as well as in other families. My given name at birth was Anne Alma Savarino. Women stayed at home to raise their children and maintained a loving home atmosphere for their husband and children. Men were considered to be sole providers for their families. In those days, income from one person for a family was sufficient and lifestyle was moderate and simple. We were taught to respect our elders and children were thought proper mannerism and edict parenting to socialize with other people.

Respect for another was the utmost trait required in family life, personal life, and also in the workforce life. Whether you were a laborer in a work field with a regular job or a career-oriented person in a professional field, or an entrepreneur with a business of your own, respect between one another, with co-workers, employees, and friends was respected and honored. Socializing with one another was exciting and a great learning experience that increased our knowledge and understanding in human nature and having compassion with one another. We are all alike and not much different in our endeavors and desires. Even our tribulations and our accomplishment in life are quite similar, but in different aspects, timing, and mashing individual choices of where our pathway leads us.

Of course, through the next levels of decades – 1950 to 2020 – women have become a strong influence in the work field as well as providing a second income while still being able to maintain a solid home life for their family. Men have learned to share responsibilities with home life as well as washing outside the home with their jobs and career. Women are now considered on an equal status as man in position at work and equal pay. Some women earn more than men in wages, depending on the job title, experience, and qualifications required for filling certain job positions. In regards toward childcare for both parents working, when it comes to pre-schools then a daycare center is available… nursery schools and grandparents that are retired also help out their families in today's world; you require two incomes to maybe get a good, comfortable living. My parents both worked and my grandmother, Maria, raised me and my brother.

Personal History

My father, Steve, was born in a small town in Czechoslovakia. He had 12 brothers and sisters. His family owned a butcher's shop and a grocery store. They also owned their own farm with livestock: cows, pigs, chickens, roosters, and horses. My father's family was situated comfortably.

My mother, Alma, was born on a small island of the black sea, the Island of Unye. She lived in the country of Yugoslavia, after World War I in 1918, which was previously under the name of Kingdom of Serbs, Croats and Slovenes. Official language was Serbo-Croatian. Macedonian and Slovene were also spoken. Capital of Yugoslavia was Belgrade. Three main islands: 'Mali Lošinj,' Veli Lošinj, and Unije are a part of chain of islands on the Adriatic Sea.

After World War II, they were also under Italy. Italian became one of the official languages as well.

Both my parents immigrated to Canada after World War II.

Family Background

Both my parents worked and provided a modest living for our family. My grandmother, Maria, raised my brother, Steve, and me. She was living with us. We spoke three languages in our household. They were Italian, Croatian, and Czechoslovakian. No one spoke English. I was two years older than my brother, Steve, and I started school when I was six years old. Since I did not speak the English language, my teacher kept me after school to tutor me in English language. I would then precede to teach English to my parents and my brother Steve. With time, we all learned to speak English and read books. To this day, I can still speak Croatian, Italian, and Czechoslovakian as well as English. My brother, Steve, can only speak English and never had interest in learning the other languages. When he was younger, he comprehended when someone spoke to him but once he learned English, the other languages were lost in his memory.

Religious Beliefs

Our religion is Roman Catholic and we were raised on their ethics and guidelines. But our family was unique because we never allowed our Catholic religion to interfere or present us with issues preventing us from attending other religious denomination gatherings. This gave us an opportunity to increase our knowledge and understanding of other religions. In the end, we are all praising one same God under different roofs but all uniting as one. Something to think about, we were always wondering about why certain ethnic groups of women were wearing *burka* – acial covering because of their religion. Certain people feel they should not go outside of their home or at work or even drive a car. Well, we should not criticize them for their beliefs or judge them for their religion. Since the Covid-19 virus, we are required to wear facial masks and gloves everywhere for our protection. Sounds familiar – definitely something to think about!

Friends

As I was growing up, my family life and my personal life was filled with so many friends from different cultures. My given name Anne Savarino was translated in different views. There are four ways of saying Anne in different languages. For instance, 'ENNI' in curation, Anna in Italian, Anike in Slovakian, and Annie in English.

I was involved in volley ball team. I also played on female baseball team. This is where I met a lot of my friends. I enjoyed figure skating as well. Sports were a good means for me in getting to know more people. There was also plenty of dances and social functions I attended that allowed me to mingle with people. The same people my family associated with were also friends with Vince, my future husband, and his family. We traveled in the same circle of friends.

In this particular time in my life, I was not acquainted with Vince or his family.

When I was 12 years old. I was rich with a very bad virus that developed into pneumonia. My lungs were full of fluid, and they started to collapse and breathing was very difficult, with shortness of breath. I had a fever that was very high – 102 – and no appetite. They rushed me to the hospital for treatment. I went into a coma for four days. During this time, I was in intensive care unit, where a large oxygen tank covered my whole bed that allowed me to breathe. The nurses and doctors were able to stabilize my vital functions, and I came out of the coma with no repercussions.

During my stay at the hospital, they had no room available for me in the children ward, so they placed me in a room in the adult ward, and I shared this room with a lady. Of course, every night around eight o' clock, the nurse would pull the curtains around my bed, so I could go to sleep. At night, I would hear visitors after eight o' clock coming to see the lady in my room. The lovely lady's name was Theresa and we become very good friends while I was at the hospital. Theresa could hardly speak English and only knew Italian. Since I knew how to speak Italian frequently, I became her interpreter, conveying conversations between the nurse and Theresa. During my stay at the hospital, I became better acquainted with Theresa, her daughter, Maria, and some of her family. Theresa was very proud of her family.

Theresa did mention she had a son, too. His name was Vince and he was two years older than me. I never met her son during my stay at the hospital because he would come after visiting hour with his father to visit his mother. Since my curtains were closed at eight o' clock, I never met him.

Social Life

When I was 13 years old, my parents allowed me to go to the movies with my friend Maureen. This was my first experience of going somewhere without my parents. I was not allowed to date or be around boys by myself. My friend Maureen and I shopped around the stores at the shopping center first and then attend the movie theater. When the movie was over, I mentioned to her that I would call my father to come and pick up us outside the front door of the shopping center. I called my father and he said that he would pick up us in 30 minutes. As we were waiting for our ride, Maureen mentioned she just needed to go in one of the stores to pick up an item she forgot to buy. So, I told her to go ahead and I would wait for my father. I knew my father would be a while till he could get here to pick us up.

As I was waiting, I happened to look through this large window in the grocery store. I noticed this handsome young man bagging grocery for customers at the cashier. He was a gorgeous-looking man that I could not take my eyes off him. First time in my life, my heart was stirring and leaping with so much excitement. I had to catch my breath in order to breathe.

I did not want to leave and I felt like I never wanted this moment to end. I felt happy, warm feelings throughout my entire being that I even feel today. I was so drawn in by this young man that it felt like time and this world stood still for this encounter. Then this young must have felt someone was watching him and turned towards the window that I was looking through and our eyes met for a brief moment. We smiled at each other. Then I heard my father call my name – Anne.

He said, "What are you looking at? I have been calling your name several times and you did not respond. Is everything okay?"

I just basically told him I was trying to see if there was a clock in the grocery store to see what time it was and I told him I did not hear him call me.

I had to think of something quick to tell my father so that I would not get into trouble and be grounded. In my heart, I did not believe my father believed my excuse of not hearing him calling me. I never saw that young man again. I kept myself busy with school, sports, and family. My social life was busy with family get-togethers, dances practices, and sleepovers at my friends. Two years just flew by and I turned 15 years old.

That is when my whole life and world changed in a complete circle of a new advents.

Family Life

My parents' social circle of friends was quite enormous and they were always in contact with one another. My friend was always included in my parents' social circle as well. My parents planned a European holiday for our family trip in the summer of 1966. Family of Vince – my husband – also planned a European holiday for their family trip for the same year – summer of 1966. Because both families had the same mutual friends, that is how my parents knew that both families would be in the Europe at the same time in the 1966. Of course, I still had not met my future husband, Vince, as of yet.

Bu Destiny had planned for our paths to cross here.

While we were in Rome, Italy, my parents took my brother, Steve, and me on a beautiful scenic adventure of Rome. My parents met each other in Rome while they were waiting to immigrate to Canada during the World War II era. My father went walking along the busy streets in Rome when he noticed a beautiful, dark-haired, tall, slim woman standing at the marketplace across the street. This woman was my future mother. It was love at first sight. My mother was so beautiful with not only dark brown shoulder-length hair, but she also had olive-toned tan skin with smooth, lovely complexion and gorgeous dark brown eyes. My father said my mother had a beautiful figure like the movie star Sophia Loren, who was quite popular at that time, and Sophia Loren was just completing a movie with the actor Marcello Mastroianni called 'Marriage Italian style' in 1964. 'Sophia Loren' was born in 1934 in Rome, and when she was a young teenager, she began appearing in films both in her native land, Italy, and later in other countries abroad. Her first major breakthrough was a film called *AIDA, The Gold of Naples,* 1953. My father was so taken by my mother that he offered her an apple to break the ice so he could meet her and talk to her. My father courted my mother for two months before he proposed marriage to her.

They married in Rome, at one of the churches, and have been together happily for 68 years till God called them both. When we were in Rome, my parents introduced us to the priest that officially married them. This priest took my brother, Steve, aside for talking to him and prayed that he would have a successful life in business endeavors and find a lovely girl to marry and have a family of his own one day. My brother, Steve, was 13 years old at this particular time. Then the priest proceeded towards me and pulled me aside and prayed that I would meet a handsome young Italian man and marry him. The priest asked God to bless me in my marriage with this young man and have a beautiful, loving family with him to complete my life with true love and happiness. The priest also hoped and wished that my future husband would return to Rome so he could meet with us and our family.

During our stay in Rome, we visited the Fountain Trevi.

This is a mystical fountain that grants special wishes. My brother, Steve, threw a coin into the fountain and made a wish. He never told me what his wish was. I myself threw two coins into the Fountain Trevi and made my wish. They say if you make a wish, you should throw the coin in the fountain to make the wish come true – the first coin for your wish and the second coin is to seal the deal in making it come true. I did not know what my brother wished for, but I wished that I would meet this wonderful, handsome, young Italian man and have a lively, happy, successful life together with him – exactly what the priest that married my parents wanted for me.

Future Desires

We left from Rome the next day for Croatia, Yugoslavia. We visited my great grandmother 'Maria', and great aunt 'Margarita'. There were plenty of relatives on my mother's side to visit in between sightseeing all the beautiful historic scenery and learning all about Croatian culture. It was quite impressive. The people were very friendly and helpful towards tourists and made us feel like a part of their families and culture. We visited a friend of my mother; her name was Reena. They were best friend from grade school since they were eight years old. Reena lived in a small city called 'PULA'. The next day, we went to visit a cousin of my mother. They both grew up together and were born on the island of 'Unije', on the Adriatic Sea. We spent the entire day with her cousin 'Amelia' and family. Amelia was my third cousin 'Emily's' mother. Before we were ready to leave, Amelia asked me if I could come upstairs to her daughter's bedroom. Of course, I said yes. I sat myself on the bed and she went to the closet. Amelia asked me how old I was, and I told her I was 15 years old. Amelia pulled out from the closet a Georgiou's white wedding dress that belonged to her daughter Emily when Emily married her love John. I was speechless and surprised that I could not say anything for at least five minutes. As I was trying to compose myself, I heard footsteps coming up the stairs. My mother stood in the doorway totally shocked and very upset. My mother informed her cousin that no way was I ready to get married now at my age or even accept this wedding dress as a gift. Amelia apologized to my mother and told my mother she was only thinking about beeping the wedding dress to pass down within the family. We left shortly afterwards but in good terms with Amelia and her family after the incident. My future goals were to finish school and select a career in the business sector.

I was thinking of maybe pursuing a career as a legal secretary as a medical receptionist. Marriage was furthered in my mind. I was too young and wanted to experience life adventures and travel. We left Croatia and boarded a ferry to take us to the island of Unije. There we would stay for one week. The house we stayed at was my grandmother Marrie's house where my mother, my aunt 'Marrie' and my uncle 'Matter' were born and raised. My great-grandmother, Maria, who was 92 years old was staying in a senior home and we had a chance to visit her as well. She was still of a sharp mind and recognized us when we entered her room. This was a blessing for her that she had constantly prayed to see us one more time before God called her to come home to heaven. Her prayers were answered because she not only got to see us but also one week later, she passed away with happiness and is in heaven with God.

Unije was a small island with only 800 people at that time in 1966. Fishing and farming were the only industry at that time. Today 'Unije' has become a vocation spot for tourists and is more modernized with technology-updated hotels plus resorts and restaurants.

I was able to connect with all my family members on my mother's side. I made new friends as well, while attending beach parties and get-togethers held in local restaurants. I enjoyed this particular island for its scenery and the beautiful beaches it had. Plus, I was able to learn more about my mother's side of the family. We also visited by boat the other two nearby islands. One was called 'VELI LOŠINJ'. 'MALI' means small island. 'VELI' means big in the Croatian and English language. These three islands, Unije, MALI LOŠINJ, and VELI LOŠINJ are all part of a group of thousands of islands located on the 'Atlantic Sea.' There were family members we met on these two islands as well. Our experience in Yugoslavia was an extraordinary adventure. We enjoyed tremendously.

Childhood Adventures

As a child, I was always very curious, ambitious, and adventurous. Having these qualities was exciting but it got me into plenty of trouble. My brother, Steve, and I would cross the railroad tracks to go fishing for 'Poly Wogs'. We would take our chances crossing the tracks when trains were already heading our way. We would wait until the last minute to cross just as the 'conductor' blew the train whistle. To get to the railroad station, we would need to cross a very busy highway that was at that time in the 1960s only four lanes. It was called HIGHWAY 401 and the same highway today is now eight lanes wide. It was renamed HIGHWAY OF HEROES here in Ontario, Canada. Sometimes we would take hikes through dense bushes and swamps areas looking for 'blood suckers' and do some fishing in clear ponds as well.

One time, I was all dressed up with a beautiful dress and Sunday shoes, ready to go to church. My brother and I decided to go to a nearby creek beside our house while we were waiting for my mom and dad to get ready for church. Without their permission, my brother and I preceded towards the creek. That was a big mistake because I lost my balance and fell into the creek and lost one of my shoes in creek. When I went home, my parents were very upset. Of course, they grounded me for a couple of days. Another time, my father was working around his 1954 Chevrolet car and he left his 1954 car keys in the ignition. Of course, my brother and I thought it would be fun to start my father's car. Our mistake was we shifted the gear to reverse and the car went backwards into the backyard. My brother was sitting in the driver's side and myself in the passenger side. We both panicked like kids do and jumped out of the car. It was lucky my father was nearby and managed to jump into the driver's seat to put the gear shift into park. My father saved the car from crashing into the fence in the backyard. My brother and I panicked and locked ourselves in the bathroom in the house. We thought we would be safe from punishment and give our father a chance to cool off his anger. When my father entered into the house, he headed towards the bathroom door and requested us to open the door. We both refused his request. He insisted we opened door as soon as possible. We told him only if he promised not to punish us. All of a sudden, everything went silent for 20 minutes. My brother and I thought we were in the clear. Naturally, my father returned with his tools and proceeded to unhinge the bathroom door. My brother and I panicked again and we were trying to figure out how to escape. Since there was a window in the bathroom and we were on ground level, I pushed my brother out of the bathroom window and he ran for safety. Unfortunately, there was no time for me to escape through the window. My father took the door down and I was punished. As far as my brother was concerned, my father was waiting for him to come home. My brother arrived home late around seven o' clock and my father surprised him by being at the door of my brother's bedroom. He could not escape his punishment.

My mom used to tell me that I should start acting like a young lady and not like a Tomboy. She did not want me climbing trees and to stay of getting into mischiefs. My mom used to say that no boy would even want me with scratches, business, and scar marks on my legs. It was time to grow up and act like a young lady. She also requested I dress like a young lady and wear chesses, not pants all the time. My mom purchased whole new wardrobe for me consisting of dress shirts, blouses, and new shoes to change me completely and she succeeded. After all, she was right because I was 13 years old and physically changing into a young woman. My body was developing and I looked more like 18 years old rather than my age of 13. I suddenly noticed that even young boys and men were noticing me more than ever. It was time to accept this new development in my life. Since my body developed quickly into a young woman's appearance, this made my parents worried, since I was still only 13. I was used to wearing loose, comfortable clothing and nothing fancy. Both of my parents were more protective of me, and I could no longer hang out with my brother and his friends. This new change of lifestyle upset my brother and myself emotionally. My brother always looked at me as a good friend as well as a sister. We enjoyed hiking, fishing, and just hanging out. This whole new outlook changed our relationship tremendously. We no longer experienced or shared the same interests. He had his friends and I had my own new friends.

Teenage Experiences and Ambitions

My teenage years were very exciting with new adventures to experience. My parents were very strict and did not allow me to date. When I was around my friends, I never let them know how strict my parents were, especially when it came to boys. I attended overnight sleepovers with my friends and certain parties that my parents did not know about. There were teenage dances held at a place called Red Barn. My friends and I would go to skating arenas and roller skating auditoriums to hang out. Especially when there was birthday party held for some of my friends' boys, they were not allowed to drive me or walk at home. I was offered rides and invitation to go to see movies on a date with certain boys. I defiantly turned down each request for a date. My parents would be very upset with me if had accepted the offer and definitely would have grounded me from seeing my friends. My mom and dad were very good parents, who were concerned about my wellbeing and safety. They were very old-fashioned in their point of views. On my 14th birthday, my aunt Mary, my mother's youngest sister, brought me my first pair of jeans, which I wanted so much.

My mother would never buy me a pair of jeans because she did not like the look of them and considered them not suitable for a young woman. Anything tight, body hugging in pants or dresses, were considered too provocative. Nonetheless, my mom was not impressed with my Aunt Mary buying these jeans. My Aunt Mary came to my defense and my mother learned to accept the fact that I loved my jeans, and I wanted to wear them.

Since my physical appearance made me look like I was 18 years old rather than 14 years old, I attracted plenty of attention from boys my age and men in the age of 20s. Even when I would walk home from school or from my friends' house, many males would honk their car horns to attract my attention and offer me rides home or try to get my phone number for dates. I ignored them and their flirting comments towards me. But that made matters worse because these men would follow me each day, and I did not want them to know where I lived. This made me feel very uncomfortable and scared. So, I decided to walk home with my friend to be safe. One day, a young man parked his car on the side of the road near the sidewalk where I was walking with my best friend Shirley. He stepped out of his car and headed straight towards me. When he approached me, he grabbed my red silk scarf and pulled it off my neck. He then proceeded back to his car and placed my red scarf around his front rearview mirror. There were three other men in his car at that time. Shirley and I figured that were friends to this young man. I had asked for my scarf to be returned to me but this man told me he would only give it back if I would go on a date with him. This person was a complete stranger to me and he looked more like a 22-year-old guy. This happened on a Friday afternoon after school while Shirley and I were walking home. He said his name was Will, and somehow, he knew my name was Anne.

I defiantly never gave him my name and that was the first time I met him. I was kind of surprised by this whole incident, and I never told my parents about it. Monday morning when I went to school, the Canadian flag was lowered at school. In my class, there was this girl I knew and her name was 'Patty' and everyone was trying to comfort her because she was in tears and very upset. I was informed that her older brother, 'Will', was in a car accident on the weekend in serious condition and was in critical condition in hospital. 'Will's' two best friends were in critical condition as well.

'Will' passed away the next day because his injuries were severe. His two friends recovered from their injuries, months later. Patty's brother 'Will' is the same man I met on Friday afternoon and he was the one who took my red scarf and asked me out for a date. I was now devastated to hear this bad news, and I knew how he knew my name. It was because his sister Patty told him. Patty knew that her brother 'Will' was interested in me and her brother told her that he took my red scarf to put in his car. 'Will' was hoping I would go on a date with him and get to know each other better. Patty said that 'Will' had my red scarf with him when the accident happened. I gave Patty and her family our condolences as well out of respect. I felt that this was the saddest day of my life. Even till today, that brings tears to my eyes when I reminisce on this memory. I realized that things happen in life that are beyond our control. My ambitions completely changed my outlook on life. I started to take life more seriously. I set goal for accomplishing better grades in school, being more responsible for my choices that I make in life, plus knowing my parents' wishes and respecting the guidelines they set for me. The season for all this change is because I realized you cannot take life for granted and you need to appreciate each day that 'GOD' gives us and live life to the fullest. Patty and her family sold their house and moved away. I never heard from her since.

Relationship Adventures

As a young teenager of 15 years, I attended many social functions with my parent. In the fall of 1966, there was a special Italian dance for a benefit being held at the Italian club in the city of Oshawa near our hometown Whitby. My parents asked me if I would like to attend this dance with them and that I could bring my friend Shirley with me for company. Of course I said yes because of my passion for dancing plus it was a night out. That night was about to change my whole life. I entered the hall and headed straight to our table where my mom and dad's friends were sitting and waiting for us.

On the other side of the hall from where we were sitting, I noticed this handsome young man staring and watching me and admiring my moves while I was dancing. Even when I was just sitting at the table, I could feel him looking at me. My friend Shirley said, "Anne, I think he likes you and is interested in asking you to dance." I was blushing and hoping he would. This good-looking young man preceded towards our table and my heart was jumping with excitement, and I was hoping he would ask me for dance. As he approached closer to us, I felt a *'Déjà vu'* feeling that I had seen him before when he came to our table to turn to ask my friend Shirley for a dance and passed by me. I felt devastated and my heart sank. Any happiness I felt just left my body and left me wondering why he asked my friend to dance instead of me.

They returned to the table after one dance and then he turned towards my parents and asked them for their permission to dance with me. I was so surprised and that warmth was exciting my body.

I was also surprised that my parents said yes to him. He led the way to the dance floor and before I left the table, my mom pulled me aside to tell me not to give him my name, address, or phone number. I replied, "Fine." He reached for my hand as we went to the center of the dance floor. I felt like I was in the heaven, and I never wanted this night to end. He told me his name was Vince and he lived in Oshawa. He then asked me what my name was and where I lived. I told Vince my name was Anne and I lived in a small town called Whitby. We exchanged our phone numbers as well so we could phone each other and keep in touch. Everything my mom told me not to do went right out the window. Vince and I danced every dance together and we never sat down once at our tables. We both forgot about our families and friends. It felt like we were the only ones in the world at that moment in time. Vince had mentioned to me that he never attended any dances with his sister, Maria, and brother-in-law. They always invited him but he always refused. This particular time he said that, for some unknown reason, he felt an urge to go to this dance. His sister, Maria, was 13 years old then. She persuaded Vince to go. Without mentioning anything to Vince, she had invited this Polish couple and their two daughters to come to the dance. Vince told me he was not impressed with his matchmaking dates his sister Maria set up. Vince never danced with their two girls that night. Vince and I were in each other's arms all night long until the dance came to an end at 12 o'clock midnight. My parents and Vince's sister were shocked that all night we did not return to our tables. There would be times when we would still be dancing even when the music stopped. Those were slow dancers with love songs; it felt like that world stood still and we only had eyes for each other. We both felt like we were on cloud nine, only responding to each other's voices and losing ourselves in each other's eyes and in each other's embrace. Vince told me he felt a warm, exciting feeling towards me that made him happy and he wanted to get to know me later. He told me that he never experienced this emotion with anyone else before. Especially only when meeting someone for the first time, I had felt the same way towards Vince. An old person told him that I was very happy too. I was 15 years old but we were quite mature for our ages and we both knew what we wanted in life. He was so handsome and resembled 'Elvis Presley'. When the dance was over, Vince escorted me towards the exit door and my parents, his family and my friend Shirley were right behind us. All the other people were getting ready to leave as well. Just before we reached the exit door, Vince stopped and turned towards me and gave me my first lingering 'kiss' on my lips. We halted the group of people: my parents and his family behind us. The surprised look on their faces was priceless and they were shocked. It definitely is true that 'DREAMS,' 'WISHES,' and the 'MAGIC OF LOVE' at first sight does come 'TRUE.'

First Love Encounter
and Experience

Vince phoned a few days later to talk to me. My mother answered the phone only to discover that it was Vince waiting to talk to me instead of a phone call she was expecting for her. My mom thought it was Aunt Maria, her sister, calling. When Vince requested to speak to me, my mother responded, "What do you want with my daughter Anne?" Vince replied that his interest in me was only to talk to me and be friends, totally innocent gesture and respect towards her daughter. My mother then handed the phone over to me. She instructed me to tell Vince not to phone here again. I responded to my mother that if she wanted that request, I suggested that she should tell Vince herself. I told my mom I wanted Vince to phone me anytime he wanted to. I too wanted to get to know him and be friends. Vince had listened to all my conversation with my mother. My mother was used to getting her way with everyone, only this time I was not going to let her have her way with Vince and me. I never stood up to my mother before as even to go against her wishes, but this time I had the courage to stand up for myself and tell her what I felt and wanted. When I talked to Vince on the phone, he was so happy that I wanted to see him and get to know each other better. We would talk about everything, including sharing our thoughts and feelings about each other. We both discovered we had a lot in common, our interests were very similar, and we liked the same things. Our certain dislikes were similar as well. We both felt so connected and comfortable with each other. Vince would call me every night during the week and twice a day on Saturday and Sunday. Vince's family and my family would wonder what on earth we had to talk about all the time. We both became very close with each other and also very good friends. Whenever I'd have a problem with our parents as family members or even with co-workers, friends or life in general, Vince and I wanted to always share our emotions and feelings with each other. We were understanding and showed great compassion towards each other's feelings and personal needs. For the first couple of weeks, we would just talk on the phone without seeing each other. Then Vince wanted to come and visit me at my parents' house and spend some time together. At first when I asked my mom, she was reluctant. Eventually, she gave in and allowed Vince to come and see me. Of course the whole family would be there too. It was Saturday afternoon when Vince came over for dinner and a visit, my mother figured it that Vince came for a visit and he might as well stay for dinner too. I helped my mom prepare a special dinner for Vince and my family. Vince met everyone in my family including my brother, Steve, and my grandmother, Maria. After dinner, I helped my mom to clean up and Vince got acquainted with my dad and my other family members. They all admired Vince and respected his values as well as his personality. They found him very respectful, compassionate, and understanding towards others. Also, they found him to be very kind, courteous, and a real gentleman. Vince was always a hard worker and he saved every penny earned. Vince also helped his parents buy their first house. Vince was 17 years old and worked as a postal worker for Canada Post Office when he left school. Vince had a fulltime job with excellent benefits, future government pension plan, and a promising future.

Vince would come and visit me every day seven days a week for six months straight without taking me out on a date. My parents were very strict. Vince and I would talk on the phone every night before we both went to sleep. We never ran out of things to talk about. Vince had a lot of patience. It came to my parents that we always shared our experience and emotions. When it came to our feelings, I still was not allowed yet to leave the house alone with Vince but we always shared kisses and hugs with each other when no one was looking and enjoyed quality time together.

Emotions and Desires

During our six months of courtship, we learned a lot about each other and what we were looking for in our future goals. Vince showed plenty of patience, compassion, understanding, and love towards me in not being able to take me out on a date with just the two of us. Vince's sister, Maria, and his family invited me over to their house for dinner. They wanted to meet me, the girl who Vince was so infatuated with. Apparently, Vince told his family all about me and my family, who were also European with Italian background. Vince also expressed he really liked me and started to have loving feelings towards me. Our relationship was getting pretty serious. Vince's sister, Maria, phoned my mother to see if I were allowed to come over her house for Sunday dinner with her family. To my surprise, my mother said yes. That was exciting news for Vince and myself. When Sunday arrived, I was so excited and nervous all at the same time; I realized I had to compose myself and stay calm. I wanted to make a good impression for his family. I loved Vince very much, and I wanted him to be proud of me, the woman he fell in love with. During the six months, our emotions and feelings changed from just being friends to a love relationship as a couple. Vince always respected me and never took advantages of our relationship. I heard Vince's car pull up in the driveway. Vince came to the front door. I went to his car. Vince drove a 1957 black Chevrolet just like the car 'Patrick Swayze' drove in the movie *Dirty Dancing*. Vince's car also had 'THRUSH MUFFLERS' for heavy-sounding take over. We took our time getting to his sister's house, stopping every once a while to hug and kiss. It was the first time we were alone and we took advantages of this special time we had together when we finally arrived at his sister's house. Vince parked his car and gave me a long, lingering kiss. Then we went into the house and Vince let me go first down the basement stairs into the family room where his family met me. They were so happy and they recognized me and knew my name. I was the young girl, 12 years old, that shared a hospital room with Vince's mother, Theresa. I knew everyone there and proceeded to talk in 'Italian' with them. Vince was so surprised and shocked to know that I knew his family, and I was able to speak Italian fluently. We certainly had an enjoyable day with his family, reminiscing our past experience.

I met all of Vince's family that day. His Aunt Raso and Uncle Pino included me in a number of family games and taught me to play cards with Italian cards. I listened to all their Italian music that I was familiar with already because as a child, I grew up in a household that played Italian music all the time. After dinner, there was some entertainment. We sat in the living room so his family could get to know me better and what my endeavors for my future were. I complied happily to all of their questions. Both my family and Vince's family were loving, caring, and very family-oriented people. Both of our families would have up to 20 family members every weekend, for dinner and family functions. Vince became a part of my family functions and I would also be a part of his family functions. Both Vince and I were surprised to know that the friends my parents hung around with were also the same friends his parents and Sister Maria associated with; what a small world or could it be 'DESTINY'? We also attended parties and picnics in the summer with both sides of the families together. It was wonderful to see everyone getting along and enjoying themselves. My parents even rented a cottage during summer months so we could be all together as one big family. We even traveled to the United Stated for vacations together. Vince and I had been together for two years at this particular time and our love was growing stronger each day. In the month of April, Vince and I were sitting the porch of my parents' house and playing a games of cards. Vince laid down his cards on the table and looked into my eyes and asked me for my hand in marriage. I definitely responded yes and jumped off my chair and threw myself into Vince's arms. Our lips met with a lingering kiss as we embraced. There is an Italian song of love that Vince and I both loved. It goes: *"CON UHA PICCOLO BACI TU E FATTO MEI A MORE CONTE."*

TRANSLATION: "WITH ONE SMALL KISS, YOU MAKE ME FALL IN LOVE WITH YOU."

"Vince, *TU SEI SEMPRE NEL MIO CUORE!*"

TRANSLATION: "Vince, YOU ARE ALWAYS IN MY HEART!"

It was a dream come true, and I wanted to spend the rest of life with Vince. Vince and I decided that it was that time to inform our parents. This was not going to be an easy task in telling them that we wanted to get married, reason being that I was 17 years old and Vince was 19 years old.

The legal age to get married, own property, and attend bars in 1968 was 21 years old, plus we wanted to get married in July 27, 1968 – only three months away from Vince asking me to marry him. While Vince was working and had a steady fulltime job at the post office, I was still attending school. We knew our parents would not agree to us getting married this young. Vince and I had been together for two years, and we wanted to get married as soon as possible so we could be together and start our new life as husband and wife.

Our love was so strong and solid that we did not want to waste a single minute apart. Being experts, our desire was to be with each other for eternity. It was a Sunday night and Vince went home to tell his parents about our plan. I decided to discuss our plans with my parents after Vince left. My parents were happy with Vince being a part of my life, but they were extremely upset about plans to get married, as soon they wanted me to go to final school and choose a career for my life. My parents suggested that we wait and plan to marry in another two to three years to make sure that this was what we really wanted. This was truly what we wanted and to spend the rest of my life together with my wonderful Vince, I proved to my parents that my love for Vince was true and sincere, and Vince felt the same devotion and the same intensity of true love for me. We planned to be together forever. I mentioned to my parents I would still continue with my education even after we were married. I also told them that it did not matter if we lived in a house or apartment as long as we were together. Vince and I both wanted to take the 'leap of love' when we first met and we knew inside our hearts that we were true 'SOUL MATES' and that 'DESTINY' brought us together. It definitely was 'KARMA' that led our paths towards each other. Life has its very own way of bringing things together. Vince and I both believe that 'GOD' played a very special important role in putting us together in life with His blessings.

Vince also faced a hassle with his parents. They were happy with me and my parents, especially when it came to my education. Vince expressed his love and feelings he had towards me and that he wanted to start a future with me.

Vince explained to his parents that I would still finish my education even after we were married. It took a while for both set of parents to come around and accept the fact that we wanted to get married. They knew that Vince and I had no intention of changing our minds. Both went on to sit down and discuss our 'WEDDING PLAN' and to work together with us in making our dream come true. Wedding date was set for 'JULY 27, 1968.'

Vince and I were so happy that they came to an understanding and planned to work together. My mother arranged an 'ENGAGEMENT PARTY' for Vince and me – the gathering of both families to share our special day and to celebrate my 17th birthday as well. Vince's mother and my mom did all the cooking in preparation for our 'ENGAGEMENT PARTY'. Vince's sister, Maria, was a great help as well. The day before the party, Vince took me to a jewelry store and we both chose our engagement and wedding rings. I was always a hard worker and saved every penny that I earned from my jobs that I had after school. This enabled me to pay for Vince's rings and he paid for my rings. The engagement party was set on my birthday, JUNE 6, 1968. Vince presented me with three gifts on my birthday. The first gift was a beautiful bouquet of long-stem 'red roses', 12 of them. The second gift he bought me was a beautiful 'GOLD-LAMINATED BIKINI' that I wanted and loved since I saw the actress in 'JAMES BOND'S' movie *'GOLDFINGER'*. I always wore 'BIKINIS' in swimwear because they were my preference from a teenage sight up to the age of 60. I made sure I was always in shape to be able to wear them. The third gift was our engagement rings. After opening my birthday gifts from everyone, Vince and I exchanged 'ENGAGEMENT RINGS' with each other. We celebrated with glasses of 'CHAMPAGNE' and a sumptuous, delectable meal, that both our mothers prepared. Italian assorted pastries and a birthday cake were served for dessert along with espresso coffee. We danced to Italian music all night long. Everyone enjoyed themselves. It truly was a memorable day and night to remember and in expressing our love for each other and sharing this special occasion with our families.

Lifetime Commitment, Devotion and Happiness

This was the year – 1968 – to plan our wedding and to start a bright, happy, and loving future together as Mr. and Mrs. Vincent and Anne Savarino truly dream come true for both of us. We were excited to plan our wedding together and even do 'HOUSE HUNTING' as well for our future home. We set our wedding date for July 27, 1968. Vince's birthday was on July 17, 1968 – ten days before our wedding day. Vince would turn 19 years old and I turned 17 years old on June 6, 1968. We were both below the legal age of 21 years old to get married and even to buy and own a house. That meant my parents would have to sign for me and Vince's parents would need to sign for him in order to get a marriage license and purchase a house. For Vince's birthday, my family and his family surprised Vince with a party. He was so happy to celebrate his birthday with everyone he loved. I ordered a special gift for Vince from Italy. Vince's parents went for a holiday to Italy to visit relatives while they were there. I asked them if they would purchase for me a beautiful 21-carat gold chain and a special 'SAINT ANNE' Medallion in gold with the inscription on the back of the Medallion: *CON AMORE*.

TUA ANNA
JULY 17, 1967

Meaning in English would be:

WITH LOVE
YOURS ANNE
JULY 17, 1967

The reason I had the year 1967 instead of 1968 engraved is because that is the year when our friendship blossomed into love for each other. Our relationship became stronger and solid and our love became more sincere with true devotion for each other. I was able to save plenty of money, so I gave Vince's parents the money to purchase the necklace for me to give Vince on his birthday. Vince loved my gift of love so much that he always wore the necklace and never took it off. Vince and I were inseparable and filled with love for each other. Vince said I was his 'special guardian angel' from heaven and I told Vince that he also was my 'special guardian angel' that God blessed me with too.

The following weekend, Vince and I sat down with our parents to discuss our wedding plans and find a house for us as well.

In regards to purchasing a house for us, we needed to have either his parents or my parents go as 'joint tenancy' ownership with us only until we both turned to the age of 21 to be legal as to own our house without my parents. Vince and I ourselves saved our own down payment for a house. We were both working and had good jobs. Vince had a fulltime government job and position with Canada Post Office with good wages and health benefits also. Vince had an excellent retirement benefit that provided him a comfortable lifestyle when he was ready to retire. I was offered a fulltime position by a retail clothing company in sales. It was the same company that I worked for two years part-time position after school. Vince and I agreed to allow my parents to be our partners in purchasing a house instead of his parents. Reason for our decision was that both my parents had fulltime jobs. My dad worked at General Motors, a company manufacturing cars and trucks, and he also was a contractor in building homes, a business of his own on the side lines. My mom worked for a company called 'Dunlop Tires', manufacturing tires for vehicles. Vince's father was the only one working at the 'General Motors'. Vince's mom was a seamstress making clothes for people and offered childcare services in their home. So technically, they would not qualify for being with Vince and me on a mortgage for a house. Therefore, my parents would be the better option to qualify with us regarding a mortgage.

Within two weeks, we were able to find a beautiful house for us. It was a ranch-style bungalow. The house was completely finished, including the basements. That was done and renovated beautifully. The house had a double garage and beautiful landscaping in the front yard as well as the backyard. There were three bedrooms, two bathrooms, separate dining room, and a living room.

The house was close to school, church, and all facilities like stores, doctors, and hospitals. The price of the house was within our budget. In 1968, you could purchase a house for 18,000 dollars. This was the price we paid for our first house. A very expensive house would cost you 30,000 to 60,000 dollars. Our grocery bill would be 25 dollars for us to full carts of food. Haircuts were 25 cents and a full treatment with color and style would cost five to ten dollars. What a difference compared to our times now! Since our decision on the house was agreed to and our completion of bank approval for the mortgage as well, our offer was accepted by the vendors of the house. It was now time to prepare and make plans of our wedding day. Between both sides of our families, there were plenty of relatives and friends to invite everyone they knew to the wedding. No one will feel hurt or left out. There were plenty of people coming from United States and from Italy that wanted to attend our wedding, to share our special day. My mom booked two separate halls for our wedding day. She booked the carousel for 100 people for lunch who traveled from outside of Canada and also for people who traveled several hours to attend our wedding. My mom then booked the Genesha Hotel for 450 people who attended lunch at our wedding. This number of people included the 100 people who attended lunch at the Carrousel Inn.

The Genesha Hotel had an extremely large hall to hold all these people, provided their own caterers and bar professionals to serve the people. The Genesha Hotel also provided accommodations for people that were from out of town. All the people were invited to our wedding, all from the immediate circle of family and friends or both sides of our family. Yes, it was definitely a large and impressive wedding. Even local newspaper was interviewing and recording the info based on the events of our wedding day.

For our entertainment, Vince and I hired a live band to play at our wedding.

We had porcelain candy dish designed with hearts engraved.

Vince and Anne
July 27, 1968

As a memory gift for every guest at our wedding, our guests who attended the lunch at Carousel Inn, the menu consisted the following courses:

1. Italian wedding minestrone soup
2. Roast chicken with mashed potatoes
3. Peas and carrots
4. Breaded halibut fish with roast potatoes
5. Toss salad with tomatoes, green onions, almonds, and dried cranberry
6. For dessert: assorted Italian pastries, apple and cherry pie, Italian ice cream, minty and chocolate chips and lemon twist flavor

During the evening, our menu for our guests served at Genesha Hotel for dinner consisted of the following courses:

1. Antipasto: bruschetta with tomato cheese and prosciutto assorted cold cuts, Italian panini (BUNS)
2. Linguine with baby clams Alfredo sauce or lasagna with a meat sauce
3. Breaded meat cutlets with herbed baby roasted potatoes

4. Green beans and asparagus
5. Roast beef with mash potatoes
6. Baby beef with mash potatoes
7. Baby carrots with pears and sweet corn
8. Baked cod with garlic mashed potatoes
9. Toss salad with tomatoes onions and olives oil
10. Dessert: assorted Italian pastries Italian ice cream rose berry vanilla and chocolate flavors assorted cookies apple and cherry pies, fresh assorted fruits, and our wedding cake
11. Bar: assorted alcohol beverages assorted soft drinks assorted specialty drinks cappuccino coffee Italian espresso coffee regular coffee and assorted teas

We also had serviettes made with own names and our wedding date engraved on them. My mother also ordered crystal glasses for the head table where Vince and I would sit without the wedding party. The crystal glasses were engraved with *Vince and Anne, July 27, 1968* and our initials VA. These glasses were designed and made for Vince and me as a memory of our wedding day. It was a gift from my mom and dad. The musicians we hired were popular Italian band that was touring Canada. We were very fortunate that out close friend had connections with this band that enabled us to have them play at our wedding. Vince and I also registered ourselves in popular retail stores for people if they would prefer buying a wedding gift for us rather than give money as a gift in our wedding party we had.

1	Maid of Honor	Best Man
2	3 Bridesmaids	3 Ushers
3	1 Surveyor Bridesmaid	1 Junior Usher
4	1 Flower Girl	1 Ring-bearer Boy

The dresses for my 'maid of honor' were a rose color and the bridesmaids' were a soft sage green and the 'flower girl' was same color. My gift for my maid of honor and my bridesmaids were Pearl Necklaces and bracelets from Vince and myself for the flower girl. Our gift to her was a pearl bracelet, the joyous for the 'best man' and the usher as well as the 'ring-bearer boy' was white jackets with a red carnation on the lapel of the jackets with black handkerchief in the front pockets of the jackets. With white long-sleeve shirts and silver and black satin-finished vests and black bowties for the usher and ring-bearer boy, they wore black pants with white sashes.

Vince's tuxedo was white jacket with white long-sleeve shirt with white vest, bowtie, a red carnation on his jacket lapel, and a black handkerchief in the outside pocket of his jacket. Vince wore black pants with a white sash.

Vince had special cufflinks made with our initial 'VS' engraved on them with a 'tie dip' in stooling silver. Since he wore a bowtie the day of our wedding, he never used his tie clip. Vince also had special ordered cufflinks and tie clips for his best man and usher with their initials engraved on them as a gift from Vince and me. The ring-bearer boy received cufflinks as well as for the flowers on every table, a center piece of beautiful assortment of roses carnation, baby breaths, ferns Gardenia, and white lilies.

My bridal bouquet consisted of beautiful red roses, coral roses and white carnation, and green baby ferns with baby breath.

Bridesmaids' bouquets consisted of red roses, and white carnations with green baby ferns.

Flower girl's bouquet consisted of white and red carnation with green baby ferns.

My wedding dress was custom made for me. The dress had white bodies with scalloped petal leaf neckline in satin French face with assorted crystal beach and Seguin's embroidered on the satin and French face. The actual gown bodice full-shirt consisted of beads and Seguin with satin and French face as well. I wore white satin shoes. The dress had long sleeves with a pointed V-shaped petal there, gracefully hugging my wrists. The bodice was form-fitting, slimming waistline with a full in white satin and French face. Even the hemline was like the body's neckline. My white satin shoes had three heels. My purse was a white satin clutch with pearls and Seguin. I wore my hair up in a French twist and my headpiece was into the frame of the 'Tiara' with pearls and assorted hem stones and crystals. A beautiful French face voice was attached to the 'tiara'.

When it came to the music, our band played for our wedding pop music blues and country music for Vince and myself. Our favorite entertain was 'Elvis Presley'. We played his song and movies for our wedding song. We went mane traditionally with 'Al Martinos' song *'Spanish Eyes'* for our 'first dance' as Mr. T. Miss Savarino. But Elvis was very much a part of our life. Vince purchased tickets to see Elvis in 1971 concert in 'Buffalo New York.' We enjoyed the concert so much. When Elvis was ready to perform his last, I knew that if I wanted to catch one of his autographed scarfs I needed to get closer to the stage area, so without any hesitation, I left everyone and flew down the concert hall stairs dressed in 'Hot Pants' outfit and six-inch heels, heading towards the stage. My mind was set on just to get there and catch the last scarf from 'Elvis'. I avoided all obstacles in my way just to have a chance of catching his scarf and having a close encounter in seeing 'Elvis'. My heart was pounding that my way was clean to reaching my goal and no one was even trying to stop me. It was very strange. It felt like a number of 'angels' were clearing my pathway so I could accomplish my goal and reach the stage without anyone interfering or stopping me. Even stranger yet, Vince and I could only have tickets high in the 'Nosebleed Section' right at the top of the concert hall. So for me, to even run from our seating area towards him seemed pretty impossible, to attempt reaching the stage in time to catch 'Elvis's' last scarf but I did reach the stage in time to catch this last autographed scarf and being able to see Elvis face to face. I was so happy and could not believe that I succeeded in my goal. Then Vince and our nephew Mike came up to join me near the stage. At first, they were upset and worried about me taking off so fast amongst the crowd of people but when they had seen that I was holding a scarf from 'Elvis', their anger turned to happiness and excitement. They were also happy and relieved that I was fine and safe. From that day on, Elvis was always a part of our life. Whatever we did or wherever we went, a sense of 'Elvis' touched our life whether it was through his music and songs being played, seeing his movies, or visiting places and vacationing where 'Elvis and Priscilla' were staying; it seemed 'destiny' had intertwined our paths in life. Even to the point of living in 'Hawaii' too, it definitely was important for Vince and me to have Elvis's song played in our wedding. Even guests enjoyed themselves at our wedding and it was a memorable experience. Around 11 o' clock, Vince and I slipped away from the wedding party to go home and change into our going-away outfits to leave for our 'honeymoon' trip. Vince changed into his blue suit with a white shirt and red tie. He still wore his silver cufflinks with his initials engraved on them and they were his 'Tis Clip' to match his cufflinks. Vince wore black leather shoes with navy socks. Vince had a red handkerchief inserted in the front pocket and red carnation on his lapel of the jacket. For myself, I changed into my three-piece 'brocade' suit. The suit was light blue and white brocade material with an 'oriental-style' neckline. Also, my shirt was slim, forming a straight A-line style. The third piece to my suit was a matching 'cape' that went over the jacket to complete my outfit. The length of the cap was the same length of my suit jacket. I wore white leather shoes and had a white leather purse to match. I wore a white large brim hat with ¾ length white gloves. We made sure to have accessories with our outfits accordingly before we could leave for our 'honeymoon trip'. It was a tradition back then to stop by the wedding hall to be introduced to our guests as Mr. and Mrs. Vince and Anne Savarino and to give our speeches in thanking everyone for sharing our 'special day' together.

After accomplishing in thanking everyone, Vince and I left for our 'honeymoon trip'. Both of us planned our trips to 'Niagara Falls' and 'New York'. Niagara Falls was the capital location for 'honeymooners'. We had an amazing time for two weeks. After our honeymoon, we arrived home and we stayed at my parents' house for three weeks. Reason for that was because our house closed with final documents on August 21, 1968. We finally moved into our house the last weekend in August 1968. It took a couple of months to settle in. Vince found a second job working as an 'usher' at a place called 'Vivee Auditorium Arena'. One of the perks that came with this new job was that we were able to see the hockey frames and all the entertainment of 'rock n' roll' groups and looked for the arena. Also, there were special events like basketball and the 'ice-skating shows'. Because Vince worked as an usher seating people, everything was free for both of us. Vince and I always made sure to spend quality time together. Vince and I could talk to each other about everything, whether it was about work or family matter, personal performance, or performing to ourselves as life in general. We always had an open-mind point of view in communicating with each other, always accepted and respected each other. When it came to making decisions, Vince and I always listened to each other about our feelings and needs and helped each other to understand and have compassion towards everyone as well as ourselves. We never tried to change each other and allowed ourselves to grow and learn from each other. We had many friends as well as family members that we learned from in how to handle what life brings, not only through our own experience but also through other people's experiences. You gain much more knowledge and understanding this way about life in general, learning through trial and error, in decision making and choice. It is like having a special personal roadmap of life for us to follow.

Vince and I were always caregiver to our family members that needed help through our years of marriage together. We always traveled with family members too. We enjoyed being with our family and sharing life experiences together during the first ten years of our marriage. I finished school by attending business classes and courses while I was working at my job in a retail store. We did not travel too much during the first ten years. This was because our goal was to pay off the mortgage of our house. This was the biggest debt we had, plus we had two children to raise: our son, Joe, and our daughter, Teresa. Joe was born on November 2, 1969, and Teresa was born on June 8, 1972. Vince was busy with Joe, taking him to play hockey, and Vince was also his baseball coach for a junior baseball league. When Joe was nine years old, he joined the bay counts and Vince was a boy of count leader for Joe's support. I was best with my daughter Teresa with dance lesson ballet classes and synastries. Between both Vince and myself working and dealing with the activity our children, we always made time for ourselves in having quality personal time together. During this time, my parents retried from work and decided they wanted to live in 'Hawaii' and spend the rest of their life there. They lived for 50 years in Hawaii before they both passed away. This was wonderful; they chose Hawaii and we would send our two children every year in the summer for three months to spend quality time with their grandparents. This gave Vince and myself a chance to work longer hours during the summer months and not worry about our children being alone, since there was no school. Even as teenagers, they traveled every year to see their grandparents. Vince and I worked very hard, working extra hours so we could reach our goal of paying off our mortgage on the house as soon as possible. We were able to pay our mortgage on the house within 12 years and that was the most qualifying feeling and exciting time in our life. Finally, our biggest debt was paid. Now we had the freedom to save, travel, and enjoy our life. We decided to travel to Hawaii every year and to explore European destinations as well. It was a wonderful experience for our children to travel alone. It gave them confidence, plenty of knowledge, and made them lose their fears of experiencing new adventures in life. Our children learned how to communicate and collaborate with people, especially gaining total independence with maturity and quality learning that only comes from life's adventures and combined with solid family values and living. Our son, Joe, was nine years old when he first traveled by himself. Our daughter, Teresa, was also nine years old when she first traveled alone with her brother, Joe, who then was 12 years old. Our children traveled every year together and sometimes twice a year to Hawaii. They would not only go in the summer month but with Vince and myself. We would travel as a family to Hawaii for Christmas holiday, to get away for winter from Canada.

Through the passing years, our two children, Joe and Teresa, matured as adults and both found their soul mates and they married them. Joe has one son named, Andrew, who married his childhood sweetheart and has two children Leah and Michael.

Our daughter, Teresa, married her soul mate and they have their children, Natasha Brandon and Focal. Our daughter, Teresa, has one granddaughter 'Ashlee' from their son Brandon. Vince and I retired from work. I was 38 years old while Vince was 42 years old at the time. We sold our large two-story house and moved to Hawaii. We spent six months in Hawaii and returned home to Canada to stay six months with our children. We bought a condo in Hawaii on the Island O'ahu known us the 'Gathering Place', where everyone arrives in Honolulu. The main airport for this island is in Honolulu and is called 'Honolulu International Airport'. To see the other island, you would look for small chartered planes for flights. Our condo was located in a small city of 'area' outside of Honolulu. Our condo was on the 14th floor, looking 'Diamond Head' and 'Pearl Harbor.' We lived there for five years. We would entertain family and friends who stayed with us when they visited Hawaii. It was wonderful to share beautiful scenery with everyone. After a while, Vince and I sold our condo to a beautiful two-story house near 'Māʻili Beach'. That was a dream come true and we enjoyed the mesmerizing sunset every evening. We truly became 'beach bums' and enjoyed the beach every day. Our lifestyle became laid back and serene. Hawaii captured our hearts and love even for all the 'Hawaiian Islands'. When Vince and I did not have guests, we would take time for ourselves and town all the other beautiful Islands of Hawaii. During the next few years, my parents both developed health issues. My father developed colon cancer, prostate cancer, and diabetes. My mom developed 'congestive heart failure'. By this time, my parents were in their 80s. Vince and I were very busy being caregivers, taking them to the doctors' appointments and grocery shopping. My father passed away in May of 2011. My mom passed away in January 2018. Vince and I had to decide whether we should stay in Hawaii or turn back to Canada. As much as we loved Hawaii, we realized that we too were getting older and we knew our children would not be able to come to live in 'Hawaii' because lifestyle in Hawaii got very expensive. They definitely could not afford it. That would mean that if Vince and I even had health issues, we would have to handle it alone and live by ourselves with no help from our family, so we decided to move back to Canada to be with our children and grandchildren. Vince and I sold our house and gave all of our furniture and household items away to the shelter for the homeless and people in poverty that needed help. Vince and I have helped others in need. We always did volunteer-work building homes for the 'hesitant' families in need. We even made 'rosaries' for 'Missionaries' to give to people and churches. We moved back in the month of July and celebrated that year's '50 years of marriage'. Our children planned a surprised anniversary party with family and friends. We had a wonderful time and cherished the memories of our life together. We lived with our son for a while till we found and bought a new house. The builder was completing off the final phase of house and we were able to purchase our new house and move in within four months. We finally moved into our house at the end of October 2017. Vince and I were so happy in our new house and it took us about three months to settle in. We celebrated our first Christmas with our family in our house. We planned a European Vacation for the months of September 2018 for part of our '50 years' anniversary celebration. Our granddaughter, Natasha, and her boyfriend, Euan, and our friends Connive and Charlie who were celebrating '45 years' wedding anniversary were planning to travel with us. The places we looked to go and visit were Rome, Italy; Florence, Italy; Milano, Italy; Venice, Italy; Paris, France; Switzerland, and Frankfurt, Germany. We had a terrific holiday for four weeks. We arrived home safely. Just before Christmas, Vince and I both got sick with flu virus. We just could not shake this virus off.

Our family doctor gave us antibiotics and had us do some blood works and X-rays on our lungs. Vince also went for a colonoscopy test and had ultrasound testing alone on his stomach area. We slowly started to feel better and flu virus disappeared. We both were happy that we were better in health. When the test results came in for Vince and myself, it changed our whole life and the plans we were making for our future good together. I was diagnosed with 'congestive heart failure' like my mom and Vince was diagnosed with 'pancreatic cancer' with 40 stage. The news of our test results were so very devastating, especially on Christmas. With Vince, it was very serious, where his cancer had already spread throughout his body. They gave Vince only two months to four months to live, and they gave me only five years to live. My heart was very weak and damaged beyond repair.

My gorgeous, handsome, wonderful-looking husband Vince passed away in my arms at Horne on April 28, 2019. Vince was only 69 years old and gave us a miracle blessing. Before Vince passed away, Vince was in a 'coma' for just two week towards the end. Just before he took his last breath, God allowed Vince to open his eyes one more time to see me and look into my eyes while I was holding him in my arms. When we gazed at each other, his eyes were expressing his love for me and I virtually expressed my love to him. Vince always told me I was his 'angel' and I responded to Vince that I loved him so much and he was my 'angel'. Then I told him to close his eyes, my love, and go with God and he took his last breath in peace. Vince passed away peacefully with God and we both felt blessed to have our final moment together in expressing our love and knowing in our hearts that we will be together soon in 'heaven'. Both our hearts and minds were at peace. There will never be anyone that could take Vince's place in my heart, my mind, my body and soul, my thoughts and love in my life. Vince and I were 'true soul mates'. Our lives were blessed by God and we were destined to be together and I feel Vince's presence around me all the time. I am where he is and Vince is where I am. We are two 'souls' intertwined together as one in unity with God the Father in heaven for eternity, so no one can even take Vince's place in my heart and love, because when you have had the best man in your life, no one can ever come close to compare with my loving husband, Vince. Even when your wedding vows conclude with till death do you part, it does not apply to Vince and myself because we both felt our love and life together was for eternity.

After Vince passed away, I sold our house within six months. It was what Vince wanted me to do. We had discussed this matter before he passed away. I moved in with my son, Joe, and daughter-in-law, Lisa. I devoted my time and life to my children, grandchildren, and great-grandchildren, spending quality time with them and the rest of my family. I also enjoyed quality time with my friends and doing Valentine work, most of all devote myself to God Jesus and the Holy Family though prayer every day.

Vince and I promised each other that if one of us passed away, we would follow this pathway of devotion for our love for each other and life itself. We would always be there for everyone, providing help in their need and counseling with advice towards their tribulation in life. Everyone always come to us for advice and know we would beep their information in confidence and privacy. They felt comfortable and were at ease discussing their problems with us. Life is about this and we must enjoy every day of life that God blesses us with, living each day to the fullest and accomplishing our goals. We should celebrate life especially with our families and friends. The memories we create are for eternity and the love we feel form each other is forever in our hearts and thoughts. 'True love is there' for everyone to attain in their life. We as humans tend to overthink what real love is. Real love is pure, innocent strings and unconditional, with no strings attached. Love at first sight is real love that will be nurtured with respect, compassion, tenderness, understanding, and commitment, with true devolution to each other without changing each other's personality and having full acceptance. We should allow each other space to grow without doubt and fear.

When you have 'true love,' materialistic things and money are not an issue of importance. 'Communication' with each other in the number-one factor in building a solid relationship. It is patience, tolerance, and trust. All these factors will give you 'true love' and 'happiness'. There is a beautiful saying to remember and to always cherish. It goes this way:

True Love Poem

I am where you are
You are where I am
Two souls intertwined
Together as one
Knowing each other
Thoughts and sharing
Our true love
In unity with
God the Father
In heaven above.

Printed in the USA
CPSIA information can be obtained
at www.ICGtesting.com
CBHW081500010324
4806CB00023B/184

9 798889 109259